T0380571

# LEARNINGS

## My multi-decade spiritual and perceptual faith journey

DAVID ALLEN

WESTBOW
PRESS®
A DIVISION OF THOMAS NELSON
& ZONDERVAN

WestBow Press books may be ordered through booksellers or by contacting:

WestBow Press
A Division of Thomas Nelson & Zondervan
1663 Liberty Drive
Bloomington, IN 47403
www.westbowpress.com
844-714-3454

Because of the dynamic nature of the Internet, any web addresses or
links contained in this book may have changed since publication and
may no longer be valid. The views expressed in this work are solely those
of the author and do not necessarily reflect the views of the publisher,
and the publisher hereby disclaims any responsibility for them.

Any people depicted in stock imagery provided by Getty Images are
models, and such images are being used for illustrative purposes only.
Certain stock imagery © Getty Images.

Scripture quotations are taken from the Holy Bible, NEW
INTERNATIONAL VERSION®, NIV® Copyright © 1973, 1978, 1984,
2011 by Biblica, Inc.® Used by permission. All rights reserved worldwide.

ISBN: 979-8-3850-3452-9 (sc)
ISBN: 979-8-3850-3453-6 (e)

Library of Congress Control Number: 2024920756

Print information available on the last page.

WestBow Press rev. date: 10/4/2024

Dedicated to those who have come before and
"kept the faith" and especially to those who
will yet find their way to faith in Christ!

# PREFACE

There seems to be much confusion and misunderstanding of the Bible and God's role in our 21st Century world. While I certainly don't have all the answers, nobody on this Earth does, I do have a different grasp and appreciation than much of what I am reading and seeing all around me.

Because of that and today's tendency of people to turn away from religion they find unsatisfying or even unwholesome, I am writing down what I have come to learn over the years. I hope that it will give some of the disaffected people a new perspective and allow them to once again turn towards God, seeking His face.

What follows are my chief learnings; a spiritual worldview and some refined understanding. The most fully developed understanding I've come to over recent years.

*Bible scriptures were quoted from the New International Version of the Bible. (Copyrighted worldwide as public domain.) Copyrighted material.*

# BACKGROUND

But before I launch into this learning, I think it appropriate to give some background as to who I am and how I came to this spiritual worldview.

I am an older, retired man born and raised in the United States Midwest. As did many who were children in decades past, my family and I attended church weekly at a protestant denomination. Most of my relatives did the same, so that was normal for me and became a foundational base in my life. I remained in the church and followed that practice throughout my life until recently when health and spiritual concerns caused me to step back from attendance, but not from faith. More on that later.

As I grew in faith, I had an interest in the Bible and though I never memorized portions of it, I did read it to gain a better understanding of the God I was following and serving. That has always been a practice of mine, to better understand what was being said and taught. I've always wanted to understand, not just follow.

Unlike many, today, I did spend time reading the Old Testament (OT) as part of that quest for understanding. I reasoned that the New Testament (NT) was based on the Old and that it would be important to understand what came before and was the base, both spiritually and physically. I eventually gained the visual and spiritual perspective you get if you spread open a Bible with the beginning of the book of Matthew under your right thumb and notice what lies under your left thumb. In your left hand you have the Old Testament, which is three times the size of the New Testament in your right hand. The New Testament may guide our faith practice today, but it is built on that wealth of what has come before and which explains much of what we read in the New Testament. I don't believe we can begin to grasp the essence of the New Testament without the base of the Old.

Reading the Old Testament, gave me a view of and thirst for the history of Israel, which is so pivotal to the Christian faith today. As I read more and more about Israel in the Bible and also in history, I came to see how special a place it is and was. Both to us, and more importantly, to God. This eventually led myself and my family to relocate and live in Israel for seven years where we worked in Israeli businesses, lived in Israeli society and I even served in the Israeli army.

My career was working with computers and so it was an easy transition to do the same in Israel where I worked for an Israeli airline headquartered southeast of Tel Aviv. The airline maintained a fleet of buses that ran routes all through the Tel Aviv area picking up employees in the morning and returning them home in the evening. I lived north of Tel Aviv about 45 miles from the airport and at the extreme end of that bus route. I would board in the early morning for the approximately one-hour ride to the office and since I was one of the first to board, I was able to sit quietly by myself for the first 20 minutes or so of the commute. I used that time to read a pocket Bible, a full Old and New Testament Bible. I would read about three chapters a day, which would take me through the whole Bible in one year. Thanks to the early morning quiet-time I read the entire Bible cover to cover several times in the years I lived in Israel.

All told, I have read the entire Bible, cover to cover, seven times; some of the books many more times and many verses as part of a morning devotional uncounted times. I've recounted all of this to say that I have a good base knowledge of the Bible.

I mentioned that I haven't memorized verses, but what I find is that as I come across various topics in all manner of material, the Lord can bring a verse or verses to mind which greatly helps me to put that information into a Biblical perspective. That has been my chief aid in arriving at the perspectives I have come to understand over time and that I want to share here.

God has always used anyone He pleases to advance His Kingdom and purposes. Likewise, I often find tidbits of information or understanding that are not meant to have a Biblical connotation that will help me piece together truly Biblical concepts. Why should the God-given knowledge and insights that are throughout the world not be useful to a person trying to expand their Biblical horizons just because it wasn't spoken by a church official? That would be limiting ourselves to one wing of the library.

I understand that some who read this document will disagree with it, some even vehemently. That is part of what I am addressing here, the polarization rife in our midst that keeps us from even contemplating that there might be a fuller, more expanded, understanding that is able to include more people in the Kingdom of Heaven. Some of our beliefs have become so exclusionary that many are left out and even castigated and pushed farther away from faith. How is that pleasing to God who has said that He desires that all should be saved?

# READING THE BIBLE

L et's start with reading the Bible, since it is the basis of what is going to be presented. Several things need to be understood as you open it to read or study its passages. It was written over a period of many hundreds of years by numerous authors to whom God spoke. Even with that consistent supernatural inspiration, each of these writers was a unique individual with varied backgrounds and experiences, which come through in their writing. But make no mistake, while the authors style or character may come through in their writing, they wrote what the Holy Spirit had told and shown them, under His watchful eye! The result is God's Word, not the authors. In addition, they were all Middle-Eastern people steeped in the culture of their time and place. A key difference between those writers and us as Western oriented readers is their approach to a topic.

To them who and why was most important while to us where, what and how dominate our queries. Because of those different emphases the writer, at the Holy Spirit's leading, either included or excluded various items of information. A Bible reader must take that into account and not try to force the writing into his or her mold or timeline.

In addition, the Bible is a composite document made up of more than one subject: historical narration, the revelation of spiritual truth and principles, and prophetic statements. Together, they all serve to make God known and knowable to us. Each of these three writings has its own style and approach. The historical narration is generally straight forward laying out what happened to who and why, maybe not extensively discussing where and how types of details.

The revelation of spiritual truth and principle is by its very nature going to be unusual to us. While we have a spiritual element within ourselves, we are dominated by our physical senses until we learn how to perceive and respond spiritually. The language used here is often more esoteric, filled with analogies or parables to help us relate the spiritual concepts to physical attributes, emotions and situations we know. It is not steeped in where, what or how since it is beyond our physical senses.

The prophetic statements are going to be yet again different. These are fore-knowledge statements about what will happen often using symbols to explain. Many of those prophecies have already occurred and we can see those facts. The who and why language of the Bible doesn't always give us nice clean details to measure against and requires some amount of faith to make the connection. For the prophetic events that have yet to occur there is the difficulty of an ancient people trying to described an event that is perhaps far-future, even to us. The symbols they use won't match anything we would use and leave us grasping at meanings. Likewise, timelines are difficult to quantify with the prophetic event often tied to another future signpost event. The timelines are often presented in terms of earthly kingdoms' durations, not years on a calendar. What we can do is be aware of the prophecy and watch for the signpost event, which itself could be symbolic.

This is all to say that the Bible is a special and unique document that requires patience and insight to understand. That patience and insight is available from God and the more of the Bible you read, the better you will understand it. Lifting a verse or passage out of a limited portion of the text can be unhelpful and mis-leading. Many times, one passage will help explain another. There is a definite interconnectedness to the whole Bible which is, I believe, intended. To gain a better understanding of the Bible you will need to invest the time and effort to read it all. The reward, however, is worth it.

A final word about the Bible. It is a message that is meant to be used not just read. Of course, as noted above it has to be read and even reread to be understood. But once that is underway the power of the Bible is set into motion by doing what God says, by living the way He has set forth. James, the brother of Jesus, tells us in James 1:22-24 that the power of the Bible comes not just by hearing, but by living it out. Reading the Bible without living out the truths of the Bible is not what God intended and gives but a small benefit well short of what's offered!

# SPIRITUAL WORD / PHYSICAL WORLD

I think one of the earliest understandings we need is that there is a very real spiritual world in addition to our physical world. As modern individuals surrounded by sight and sound, science and technology, we very much focus on the physical world all around us, which has a major impact on our daily lives. We tend to dismiss the possibility of a spiritual world since we can't perceive it with our five senses and therefore often consider it at best as symbolic or just plain disregard it as Biblical fantasy.

But if you spend any time in the Bible you will come across passages of scripture that refer to this spiritual world. John 4:24 says, "God is spirit and those who worship Him must worship in spirit and truth."

That is as unequivocal a statement as you are going to read identifying a spiritual world. Other passages refer to heavenly angels or a person caught up into heaven or describe Jesus Himself ascending to heaven. If you are going to find value in the Bible, you have to accept that there is an active spiritual world.

Further, I will suggest that there is more impact on our physical world by the spiritual world than we understand. Proverbs 19:21 says, "We may plan all we want, but it is the Lord's plan that will reign." Many times, we will not see His plan until after it has reached its conclusion, considering our lack of spiritual training and perception. Our limitation does not negate His influence! And we must expect it and look for it to discover it. Most of us, of course, don't.

But how are we to do that? As God's creation, formed in His image (Gen. 1:27) we also have a spiritual element within us that allows us to perceive and communicate with God. 1 Cor. 3:16 says, "Do you not know that you are God's temple and that God's Spirit dwells in you?" God wants a relationship with us and even more wants to help us. Jer. 29:11 says, "For I know the plans I have for you, declares the Lord, plans for welfare and not for evil, to give you a future and a hope." Because of this and in order to help us, He reaches out from the spiritual world to us in the physical world, but that outreach is spiritual in nature.

Let me at this point suggest an image to help you

better visualize the spiritual world. Imagine a large solar system sized cloud that represents the spiritual world. Now imagine within that cloud an area carved out that contains our physical world. The world of spirit is all around us, all encompassing, but we can't see it with our physically attuned eyes. It's there, but not in a wavelength our eyes can see, like infrared light is beyond our vision. We may not actually be able to see God's surroundings with our eyes, but we can perceive God's spirit with help from God and by that means gain some validation of His spiritual world!

## SPIRITUAL BEINGS

Hopefully, the above has helped you move closer to the reality of the spiritual world. Now, I need to discuss the inhabitants of this spiritual world. There is of course God, His archangels and angels and even more esoteric beings like cherubs and the living creatures that accompany God as He moves about as described in Ezekiel. There are two named archangels mentioned in the Bible, Michael and Gabriel, but there certainly could be and probably are more. Named saints are also noted in heaven. As to the general population of angels, both Hebrews 12 and Revelation 5 refer to "myriads of myriads" of angels; with a myriad being defined as ten thousand. That would amount to at least many thousands and as many as 100,000,000 angels if "myriads of myriads" is multiplication (don't forget – old language).

Not all the angels, spiritual beings, are still in heaven, however. At some point, as described in Revelation 12, there was a war of rebellion in heaven the result of which was that Satan, a leader among the angels, and as many as a third of the angels were defeated and all cast down to Earth (Is. 14). Here they prowl now unseen by eyes with our limited abilities, causing whatever harm they can. Spiritual beings not only abound, but they are everywhere.

With the reality of fallen angels having been put forth, I need to address what I understand that to mean to us. These are supernatural beings with capabilities like those attributed to angels in the Bible; not someone we want to confront in our own strength. These fallen angels are opposed to God and His kingdom and want to render it a failure. They strive and have worked ceaselessly to disrupt and destroy God's kingdom in this world. They have, I think, some limits and we have some protection. In the well-known Ephesians 6 passage about the armor of God, we are told how we can resist Satan's schemes and attacks by putting on the armor that God has provided us. I would point out that this passage describes a defensive stand not an attack; open combat with fallen angels is the province of God's archangels and angels, themselves supernatural beings.

Based on the book of Job, which I think is an allegory to help us comprehend the duality of the two worlds, it is my understanding and perception that Satan and his minions can't physically harm someone who follows and belongs to God. In the book of Job, Satan is shown as having to get God's permission to test Job by physically harming him or his family. Again, at the Last Supper, Jesus tells Peter that Satan has asked to attack (sift) him. He, Satan, is not all powerful, doing as he will, even though he wants to be and wants us to think he is. Other verses throughout the Bible describe God's protection from the evil one. 2 Sam. 22:3-4, Is. 54:17, 2 Thes. 3:3, and 2 Tim. 4:18 all record the protection available from God against evil. I also think and understand that there is a component of trusting in and seeking God's protection in order to be best protected. Those who don't follow or especially those who ignore or reject God don't have His full protective help.

So how does Satan inflict and spread his evil? His best and maybe most effective weapon seems to be the lie! To convince someone of something that is not true and particularly someone who doesn't have or use the protecting clarity of God. Jesus calls Satan, "the father of lies" in John 8:44. Satan is willing to spend a lot of time, years even, to convince vulnerable people or peoples of his untruths, whether it is to harm someone he has targeted or to tear down and undermine a large group of people about a right way of thinking or doing. Looking back a century you can easily see the evidence and outcome of persistent lies and evil. Right now we seem to be in the midst of yet another big effort to substitute lies for truth.

Having stated and believing the above, I don't want it to be thought that Satan cannot try to cause Believers trouble. He does not respect anyone, including God, and will try to cause harm and trouble wherever he can. Jesus Himself said in John 16:33 that "in this world you will have trouble", whether He means each of us individually or all of us collectively, there is trouble in a fallen world. Satan can and will incite a deceived person to lash out at a believer. But we have Jesus as a helper and a shield to ward off Satan's attacks if we stay close to God. We need not walk around in fear! 1 John 4:4 "Greater is He that is in me than he that is in the world." We will be attacked, that is the nature of our world, but we also have the help and the means to fend off these attacks. Don't give in, don't despair!

So, what is the conclusion? We need to understand who both God and Satan are! We need to cling to God and use His help to resist and fend off evil! And we need to have our eyes wide open to see clearly both good and evil!

# DEBATES

There are some major debates about Biblical interpretation that have gone on for decades or even longer. I'd like to address some of these and explain my viewpoint on these issues.

## CREATIONISM / EVOLUTION

Nothing like jumping right into the deep end! The Bible makes clear, beginning on its first page, that God is the creator! It goes on to describe His creation steps; not in scientific detail or how He did it, but most notably that He did it. Remember, who and why; not where, what and how.

Against that we have the scientific theory of evolution with bones, fossils and carbon-dating to back that up. Fairly substantial stuff. And the two adherent groups have been in heavy disagreement especially since Darwin put his theory of evolution forward.

I submit that this is a false dichotomy stirred up by Satan to cause massive division and distrust. And it has worked very well! But why give in to this confusion and give the enemy this victory? There need be no conflict!

With the skeletal remains in our possession and the various proofs of timelines, it is very hard to refute that some sort of developmental progression took place unless you are willing to believe that the enemy seeded our world with fakes to delude us. I don't believe that is so! Fallen angels have had limits placed on them as discussed above and I believe this is another limit. God did not intend that we could not see His handiwork. And while I believe that Satan can and does lie to us, I don't think he is allowed to create fictitious, solid items just to trick us. He thrives on trying to mess with our minds or the minds of non-believers to use against us. He is not a creator! He is a deceiver!

So then, what to conclude. Combining faith in the Bible with the evidence in front of our faces, it seems clear that God used an evolutionary process as a means of His creation. He apparently set processes in motion that worked over long periods of time and at just the right moments caused new paths to be taken.

Let me add a little further explanation about God's

use of processes. The Bible clearly tells us that God created and established everything! Each of us and everything around us.

As I read the Bible, I understand and believe that God is our/The creator. As I have progressed in my faith, He has allowed me to understand more about His creative process.

The evidence of eons, revealed by our scientific studies and ongoing expansion of knowledge, is that each created thing from the sun, the planets and everything on Earth came about by a process, some very long. Even the creation of a new life, a baby, is a process. Nine months of development from conception to birth; followed by twenty plus years of growing, maturing and educating to reach adulthood. This is God's chosen means of creation! We see it everywhere in our daily lives. Even the Big Bang which occurred in an instant was likely the culmination of a process of drawing all the components together in such a way that the bang occurred. Then the process unfolded throughout millennia upon millennia according to the pattern God designed to result in the universe and world and people we know today. And obviously, at least to me, the pattern was kept on track to arrive at and achieve the precise result God intended. That is the creativity, power and patience of God.

These processes may seem interminable to us in our finite life spans, but as Peter wrote (2 Peter 3:8), "With the Lord a day is like a thousand years and a thousand years are like a day." We measure time, God creates results that are so vast that time is mostly irrelevant.

Returning to the topic of creative evolution, as I look at the complexity of a human being and the world in which we live, I can no more accept that this complexity and sophistication just all happened by happy accident, or the beneficial survival of the fittest every time, than I can believe that I can hover unaided in the air. I see us, our world and our universe as the miraculous result of a divinely guided process.

With the extended process of creation having been put forth, there obviously were not literal 24-hour creation days. The language of Genesis, "there was evening, and there was morning – the nth day" is symbolic of an era or eon not the literal tracking of time. God is not bound by time as noted above in, 2 Pet. 3:8b "With the Lord a day is like a thousand years and a thousand years are like a day." It is symbolic just as we sometimes say, "back in the day..." meaning a past time or era, but not a specific, single past day. When we insist on this finite time construct, we are trying to put God in a box and limit Him to our measurements and then we turn around and say He is infinite. We can't have it both ways!

As an interesting aside to this discussion, I've read that the latest advance in our brains came about 5,800 years ago with a mutation of a gene that affects brain capacity. This resulted in modern man; us. If you look through the lineages of the Old Testament that would correspond closely with appearance of Adam and Eve. God's recent creative nudge resulting in the people of the Biblical times and now us.

A further confirming note comes from Genesis 4, the story of Cain and Abel. After Cain kills Abel, he is banished in verse 13 and in verse 16 he flees to the land of Nod, east of Eden. There, in Gen. 4:17-18 it says, "17 Cain lay with his wife and she became pregnant and gave birth to Enoch. 18 Cain was then building a city and he named it after his son Enoch."

There were other people out there! Taking the Bible at its word that Adam and Eve were new creations of God (with better brain capacity?), were these others then those who came before? I think so, but in any event the Bible documents other people already on the Earth.

The Genesis 2 account of the creation of Adam and then Eve is very allegorical, not physically descriptive (it is who and why). I don't see that this allegory precludes God's creative nudge that resulted in the humans that the Bible then goes on to document. Don't forget that in the Biblical narrative all of mankind, except Noah, his wife, their sons and their wives perished in the flood. With Noah being a Biblically documented descendent of Adam and Eve, no one from any other lineage survived and is now on Earth today.

I will also add a recent, confirming learning that I've had by reading a book called," Signature in the Cell: DNA and the Evidence for Intelligent Design" by Stephen C. Meyer. The author pointedly doesn't challenge the idea of an evolutionary process, but does dispute the Darwinian idea of blind, undirected biological change. We now know that DNA contains the detailed, complex code to create a human being or animal for that fact. The immense detail and complexity imply an intelligent designer. Indeed, the question that Darwinian evolution cannot answer is where did the first life come from? Especially given that life can only develop by using internal, fully developed DNA and its associated cellular "machinery", which controls all cellular growth and division. All attempts to posit how life started without a designer have been scientifically refuted. Indeed, Meyer, went to great pains to examine every non-intelligent design premise put forward; they all failed to prove viable. They are all an unsuccessful attempt to deny intelligent design by a creator God.

# FREE WILL

One of the more difficult questions to answer is why bad things happen to good people. How could God allow a bad thing to happen to a person or the world?

The answer, I believe, is God granting us free will.

God did not want automatons who were compelled to worship and serve Him. He wanted the people He created to freely turn to Him and embrace Him in a familial relationship. He has granted Himself the freedom to intervene positively; in Ex. 33:19b He says, "I will have mercy on whom I will have mercy, and I will have compassion on whom I will have compassion." God has, however, limited Himself to allow us to freely make choices, even extending to whether to follow Him or not. From the very beginning in Gen. 2:17, when God told Adam, "You must not eat from the tree of the knowledge of good and evil," He did not prevent Adam from doing so – He granted Adam (and Eve) the free will to obey or disobey. Perhaps even more explicit is the well-known John 3:16-18;

> "For God so loved the world that He gave His one and only Son, that whoever believes in Him shall not perish but have eternal life. For God did not send His son into the world to condemn the world, but to save the world through Him. Whoever believes in Him is not condemned…"

God clearly wants a healthy relationship with us, even providing a clear, simple path to Him. But He will not force it on us!

Disobedience, as we see throughout the Bible has consequences, but we are free to choose to suffer those consequences as individuals or as nations. For God to step in and personally, visibly prevent a harmful or detrimental event, at whatever level, would be to impose His will over ours! And where would that line be drawn? We would never all agree where that boundary should be and we would not be a truly free people. That's the situation – we get to be free, but we have to live with the consequences. Those consequences may be painful to God and us, but the alternative is for us to be dominated. That is not the world that God created or wants.

Coming back to the questions above, God wants us to be free, well and happy, but He has resolved that He will not force that situation on us. The dire outcomes are on us due to the choices we make! Whether it is due to deliberate acts of commission or to acts of omission, like failing to help others or to do what we can to protect from and mitigate natural disasters.

This approach, I think, is for God a "prime directive." That is not to say, however, that He wields no influence over the affairs of mankind. He does guide and lead people at all levels to do "the right thing, the necessary thing", but He doesn't force anyone! If one person is unresponsive, He can and will move on to another. He also uses people who are not particularly spiritual, but are influential and can be passionate about a cause to accomplish His purposes.

There are numerous examples over the years of people who have had great impact on our lives and even on nations and world events. Think of Winston Churchill and Franklin Delano Roosevelt. Neither one of them was particularly noted as a spiritual leader or particularly pious man, but they undoubtedly were highly instrumental in turning back what was a major attack by our spiritual enemy, using Germany, to forcibly reorder the world. On a smaller scale think of Oscar Schindler, a worldly man, who enabled many Jews to be rescued from the Nazis.

A classic example of this guiding by God is the story of Esther, in the Old Testament book of the same name, who was used to save her people. The well-known quote from Est. 4:14 says it well,

> "For if you remain silent at this time, relief and deliverance for the Jews will arise from another place, but you and your father's family will perish. *And who knows but that you have come to your royal position for such a time as this?*"

The evidence is there if we will but seek it out and give ourselves a chance to see and believe it.

# THE CHURCH

I mentioned in the background section that I no longer attend church. There are two reasons for that. But before I explain that, let me say that I wholeheartedly support church attendance, worship and fellowship! The caveat I would add is to do a thorough job of understanding what a church believes, teaches, practices and how it conducts and governs itself. Even then I would attend for a while before proceeding to membership to be sure the church is a good fit for you. You should find a Bible believing/teaching church. One that is still open to learning – not one that is locked down into rigid, dated doctrine and practices. If the ideas presented above are anathema to that church, then keep looking. Better to find a suitable faith-based church then the one nearest to your house.

My reasons for not attending are as follows. First, I am profoundly hard of hearing and a church service is a very audible event. The singing and hearing of hymns, music and lyrics, are undecipherable to me. Even with familiar hymns I can't keep track of where the congregation is in the music and verses. The liturgy, the prayers, the sermon are all unintelligible to me. You may think, just go and be in the worshipful atmosphere, but the truth is that all of these issues are a reminder that I can't participate. Even talking with people before and after the service is very difficult for them and me. Many churches can't/don't afford extensive aids for those with perceptual limitations.

Secondly, I find that today's organized, denominational church is not what I think God intended. It is built on structure and hierarchy with many dos and don'ts, locked in doctrine, power levels and monetary requirements. It seems to consist of two focuses; the spiritual preaching and teaching and the business of church. The two are of course distinct with unfortunately too much emphasis on the business side. A great deal of the church's character depends on the mindset of the pastor/priest, but the non-local higher levels of the church organization have a significant influence as well. I served as treasurer of my last church for eight years, so I had a front-row seat to observe both the local and synod activities.

A few thoughts on what is publicly evident about churches and denominations today. Most disturbing is the deviant behavior of both local and senior church officials across the spectrum of organized religion. We often hear that immoral activities have been going on for years and that the church did its best to hide the offenses and offenders while it "dealt" with the issue. But the dealing involved hiding the sin not confronting it Biblically. The Apostle Paul says in 1 Cor. 5:1–2 to "put out of your fellowship the one who does this," not hide them or the sin. If some manner of repentance follows then a measure of fellowship could be restored. But the church must be kept clean of such behavior.

Another issue is the rigid and arrogant use of doctrine to limit those in the church who the senior leadership doesn't want to have any power in the church. Even now, there is a move in a major denomination to prevent women from serving in positions of responsibility. I am not going to debate whether women can serve as pastors or not, but what's happening now is using the Bible to discriminate and restrict service. What about Gal. 3:28, "There is neither Jew nor Gentile, neither slave nor free, nor is there male and female, for you are all one in Christ Jesus."

And lastly, I question the need for the multiple denominations/hierarchies we have today. In some cases, there are notable differences in to how to approach worship. But often the differences are less significant and seem more like stubborn disagreements that resulted in separate denominations, which incidentally created more positions of power and are cause for more division among us. The enemy is surely pleased by that.

# THE MESSIAH

'␣ve written about a number of the major topics that the Bible addresses, but I have yet to write about THE major topic of the Bible – The Messiah. The Messiah is the anointed one. As I've already noted, the point of the Bible is to acquaint you with God, His world, His ways and His relationship with us.

Throughout the Old Testament we learn much about God: His nature, His directives for us to live a happy and successful life and His interactions with us. By the end of the OT, we see a world with a limited knowledge of God in general and the group He has chosen to work with, the Israelites, with a troubled, intermittent connection with Him. They consistently failed to live and abide by the covenant relationship God had established. But God didn't give up on them/ us. He made a new covenant that was much easier for us to live with and took the majority of the burden on Himself.

Obviously, He always knew how the relationship with us would progress and He had a plan to deal with that. There are many prophecies in the Old Testament about the coming Messiah – over 300, starting in Genesis. Many/most of these Messianic prophecies cannot be contrived or controlled. The odds that one person could fulfill all of these prophecies are astronomical, a number followed by untold zeroes; not achievable by any human other than the "anointed one" God sent to us as His Messiah.

The New Testament, then, is the revelation of this Messiah, who He is, what He did, where He came from and how we should live. The Bible tells us, and we can see by what He did, that He was no mere mortal. He healed people by a touch or just by speaking to them; He turned ordinary elements into something else or into much greater quantities. He more than once brought dead people back to life and, of course, He Himself, Jesus, came back to life after being crucified!

So why do we need a covenant with God? First through designated practices and now through faith in the Messiah Jesus? We've already established that God created us to have a relationship with Him, but He doesn't tolerate evil. He knows that unrestrained evil corrupts and destroys everyone and everything it touches. It respects no one and shares with no one; it is not relational and doesn't acknowledge any superior. His covenants are then a way to deal with evil, also called sin, so that there is a way for Him and us to interact, for us to get back into relationship with Him when we fail – and we do regularly fail.

So why was there an old covenant? I surmise that if Jesus had just shown up in Genesis and said, "I'm here and I'm the way forward," we would have mostly ignored Him and gone our own way as is often seen in the Old Testament. God bodily walked with Adam and Eve in the Garden of Eden, Gen. 3:8, and yet this was not enough to keep them from disobeying one simple rule. We still do plenty of disobeying today. There was then barely any knowledge of God, much less sin and the need for a Redeeming Messiah. We first needed a history with God and an understanding of His expectations and our shortcomings and tendencies. The Old Testament rules, practices and responses were our way to learn all of that. We weren't ready for the Grace relationship we now have with God.

Galatians 4:4 says, "But when the time had fully come, God sent his Son, born of a woman, born under law." So, what was this fullness? The world had proceeded to the point where there was a continent spanning government, Rome, and a widespread language, Greek, making travel, communication and understanding easier. There was a hopeful expectation in Israel for The Messiah and a growing global disillusionment with idols as a means of help – a vacuum existed. And there were hundreds of years of trying and failing under the old covenant. So, God took the next step outlined in Jer. 31:31-34,

> "The time is coming," declares the Lord, "when I will make a new covenant with the house of Israel and with the house of Judah. It will not be like the old covenant I made with their forefathers when I took them by the hand to lead them out of Egypt, because they broke my covenant, though I was a husband to them," declares the Lord. "This is the covenant I will make with the house of Israel after that time," declares the Lord. "I will put my law in their minds and write it on their hearts. I will be their God, and they will be my people. No longer will a man teach his brother, saying, 'Know the Lord,' because they will all know me, from the least of them to the greatest," declares the Lord. "For I will forgive their wickedness and will remember their sins no more."

We still have the choice to agree with, repent and accept God's covenant, but there are no more scheduled rituals to follow. (As an interesting aside, the words for repentance in Hebrew, "*poneh bi teshuva*," mean to "turn in response," as in turning back from going in a wrong direction.)

Why is Jesus the only way now? Per the covenants, sin had to be paid for; it couldn't be left unresolved. That's also the principal of all modern legal systems and law enforcement. In the old covenant the payment was usually the death of an animal substitute and a blood sacrifice; an act that denoted how serious the issue was. But a sacrifice was required for each sin and the ongoing sacrificial system clearly wasn't leading to a kinder, gentler, more faithful Israel regardless of the other changes noted above that were happening. There also was no provision for reconciliation outside of Israel. Acts 3:18-20 says,

> "But this is how God fulfilled what He had foretold through all the prophets, saying that His Messiah would suffer. Repent, then, and turn to God, so that your sins may be wiped out, that times of refreshing may come from the Lord, and that He may send the Messiah, who has been appointed for you – even Jesus."

God's solution was to come to Earth Himself, live a blameless life and then as the ultimate sacrifice, pay the price for everyone, everywhere who would accept that gift in order to inaugurate the new, better covenant. That appearance and final sacrifice was Jesus! His was the <u>only</u> needed and accepted eternal payment made once and for all people everywhere. Acts 1:8b, "… and you will be my witnesses in Jerusalem, and in all Judea and Samaria, and to the ends of the Earth." Since the old sacrifices, now abolished, were insufficient and had to be repeated every time a new sin was committed the new covenant of free grace was put in place to grant us permanent reconciliation with God. You have but to accept His Grace!

# WHAT NEXT

Given the understandings I've written about in the preceding pages, how should we now live? We would do well to live by Jesus' words in Matt. 7:12, "So in everything, do to others what you would have them do to you, for this sums up the Law and the Prophets." Most of us know this as the Golden Rule, but it was Jesus who said this and it was recognized as such a piece of wisdom that it was put forward even for secular peoples. The other guideline I would suggest is the Apostle Paul's words to the Galatians in Gal. 5:22-23, "The fruit of the Spirit is love, joy, peace, patience, kindness, goodness, faithfulness, gentleness and self-control." Living in such a manner with these attributes as goals would keep us out of so much trouble! It may be a religious text, but it, just as the Golden Rule, can apply to everyone's lives to great benefit.

So, what is the state of "religion" in our world today? I don't find a lot of either guideline above in evidence, at least in a notable amount of the public facing aspects of religion. There are certainly goodly numbers of people faithfully following the Bible's teachings and aiming to lead a more righteous life. There are also quite a few who have taken the Bible's teachings out of context and used selected verses to justify and support attitudes and actions they hold, practice and want to promote. They are demonstrably in conflict with Bible verses and principals such as Lev. 19:18b, "… love your neighbor as yourself" and John 13:34a where Jesus said, "A new command I give you: Love one another."

There is a good deal of venom put forth today and a restricting of not just who can be called righteous, but rhetoric calling anyone not following and endorsing stated positions demonic. This is the work of the enemy stampeding some religious groups into making faith and the Bible hateful. This is a lie – Satan's best tool!

# OTHER THINGS I'VE LEARNED

## WORSHIP

Hebrews 9 describes worship under both the old and new covenants. The daily temple worship under the old covenant occurred in the Holy Place, outside the curtain of the Most Holy Place where God resided. Once a year the High Priest could enter the Most Holy Place to make blood atonement for sins committed in ignorance. The way for regular entrance into God's presence hadn't yet been opened to all.

When Jesus died on the cross, the curtain separating the Holy Place from the Most Holy Place was torn from top to bottom, Matt. 27:50-51, indicating that access to the Most Holy Place was now opened. That is where we live now. We have daily access to God through prayer and for worship!

Worship is more than singing songs; it's a way of life. I think this is an important explanation/definition of Worship to help us in our lives all week, not just on Sunday. Worship is a continuous, daily decision to live in a way that brings glory to God and blessings for ourselves. Take an honest look at your life. Examine your actions, your thoughts, and your motives. Are you more consumed with living for the things of this life and what's in it for you right now, or are you focused on living for the eternal?

# THE LAST TRUMPET

The symbol of The Last Trumpet may not be a new concept, but it is one that has caught my attention and intrigued me. As such I wanted to better understand the support for this in the Bible.

The Last Trumpet is called out in 1 Cor 15:51-52 as the sign that the faithful, whether dead or alive, will be resurrected into a spiritual body.

> "Listen, I tell you a mystery: We will not
> all sleep, but we will all be changed - in
> a flash, in the twinkling of an eye, at the

> last trumpet. For the trumpet will sound,
> the dead will be raised imperishable, and
> we will be changed (raptured)."

See also 1 Thes 4:13-18. (We learn from Rev. 20: 5 that the dead from before the Tribulation didn't come to life until after the Millenium at the Great White Throne judgment. See also Matt. 25: 31-46. That must mean that the dead who are raised at the last trumpet are those who died during the Tribulation up to that event along with those alive at the last trumpet.)

What is the last trumpet? In the book of Revelation there are a number of judgments enumerated. There are three sets of seven divine judgments on the Earth with the last or third set of seven being denoted as judgments of wrath. Each set of seven is characterized by a signature event; seals opened, trumpets sounded, or bowls poured out. The second set of judgments is a series of seven trumpets and is prominently featured in Revelation chapters 8 - 11. In Rev 11:15-19 the seventh/last trumpet is sounded.

> Verse 15 "The seventh angel sounded
> his trumpet, and there were loud voices
> in heaven, which said: 'The kingdom
> of the world has become the kingdom
> of our Lord and of his Christ, and he
> will reign for ever and ever.' 16 And the

twenty-four elders, who were seated on their thrones before God, fell on their faces and worshipped God, saying 'We give thanks to you, Lord God Almighty, the One who is and who was, because you have taken your great power and have begun to reign. The nations were angry; and your wrath has come. The time has come for judging the dead, and for rewarding your servants the prophets and your saints and those who reverence your name, both small and great – and for destroying those who destroy the Earth.' 19 Then God's temple in heaven was opened, and within his temple was seen the Ark of His Covenant. And there came flashes of lightning, rumblings, peals of thunder, an earthquake and a great hailstorm."

This seventh/last trumpet clearly represents a great change! Heaven is opened and God begins active control and direction of Earth – He begins to reign over our physical world! And He rewards his servants as called out in 1 Cor 15:52! The seven-trumpet symbology of Revelation mirrors the seven-trumpet symbology of the Old Testament book of Joshua. The army of Israel marched around the city of Jerico for seven days with priests leading the way blowing seven trumpets and leading other priests carrying the Ark of The Covenant. On the seventh day the priests and the army marched around the city seven times and on the seventh time around gave a loud blast on the trumpets accompanied by a loud shout and the walls of Jerico fell down and the army rushed in and took the city. Notice that the Ark was present in both soundings of the seventh trumpet(s) and divine judgement and change was delivered.

One further important note. This event is not at the beginning of the seven-year period known as the Tribulation, but well along in this time span following the seven Seal Judgments. The remaining events after the trumpets are the seven divine Bowl Judgments of God's wrath and the Second Coming of Jesus! The Rapture of 1 Cor 15:52 could not occur after the seventh trumpet because what follows is wrath and per 1 Thes 4:9 "For God did not appoint us to suffer wrath, but to receive salvation through our Lord Jesus Christ." And there are no other sequences of trumpets in the book of Revelation. This narrows the last trumpet of 1 Cor. 15 to the seventh trumpet marking divine judgment and establishment of God's reign in Revelation.

# FINALITY

I recently finished a 28-day study on the book of Revelation. As always it was eye opening and thought provoking describing an astounding, consequential seven years of God dealing with us on Earth. It ends, however, with the wrath of God, noted above, that He has been holding back now poured out on Earth after those who have accepted Him are either called to Heaven or safely in their grave. It ends when nothing further can be said or done to convince those still alive to turn to God. Even angels flying through the air calling out to the people doesn't move them. What an astounding picture.

People for millennia have been calling for proof that God is real and here they can actually hear and see angels. And still, it is not enough! They have been so enslaved by Satan and are so determined not to yield to anyone (but of course they have) that they refuse a personal appeal from God's supernatural messengers. Even more amazing, at this time after half of Earth's current population has perished in judgments, Jesus Himself comes to Earth to lock Satan away and lead those remaining on Earth for 1,000 years. When that time is completed, and Satan is unbound for a short period a great number of those who lived with Jesus here and visible will rebel and still say they don't want Him! They would rather be free to practice evil!

At this point God ends the time of His outreach to the people of Earth and gives them what they claim they want. Eternal heaven to those who want God and eternal separation to those who don't. Proof that God has honored and strictly kept His promise of free will. Proof of His divine judgment, rewarding those who want to follow Him and sending those who insist on evil away, after many second chances, so they may no longer harass or harm the faithful. An outcome reminiscent of the Great Flood when only eight were saved, but this time a better outcome with vast numbers in heaven and leaving no doubt of wisdom versus the corrosive nature of unfettered, undisciplined, abused free will.

# CONCLUSION

I hope that these ideas and understandings expressed above help to provide some clarity in the polarized world we live in today; at least as it relates to faith, belief and repentance. I also hope that you can see the Bible as a reliable guide. Many have tried to make it say what they want it to say, but that can only succeed for a while if you let them.

Perhaps the biggest thing I have learned over the years was how much I didn't understand, how much there was still to be learned and how bound up I was in "established" thinking. I'm not saying to question everything, but at least be sure you can find Biblical support for the faith you hold. Something more than just a phrase or a single verse; rather a complete and repeated idea, approach or premise. It took, in some cases, years for me to gravitate from old, locked-in, unsupported thinking to what I have come to understand now. How much farther I have to go I don't know, but I look forward to the journey!

# ABOUT THE AUTHOR

He's an older, retired man. His family attended church weekly and that became a foundational base in his life. With an interest in the Bible, he read it to gain understanding of the God he was following and serving. In order to better understand what was being said and taught.

Printed in the United States
by Baker & Taylor Publisher Services